Howard Lull

LEADERSHIP

LESSONS

LIVED

HOWARD LULL

INTRODUCTION
THE JOURNEY

A Journey is like a Marriage. The certain way to be wrong is to think you can control it -John Steinbeck

If you read my first book *Leadership Lessons Learned* then you know investing in leaders of all levels remains a passion of mine that continues to be fueled in the fires of refinement. I continue to find that true leaders are evolving as they desire to become more. They buy books that contain information they may already know, going through the monotonous repetition of the basics to lay the foundation that ensures their success. They do this just to get it right. Leaders of all generations are realizing they need to change and grow to become the leaders their organizations need them to be. They have developed an understanding that yesterday's tools may not be what are needed today. They have forged firm foundations that have led many people through hard times as well as having provided stability during challenging times. That's not to say they haven't had failure in their lives. Even though we are all looking for a flawless leader, I have never met one. The wisest leaders understand that at times they have failed on the path to achieving some successes. That doesn't make them weak or disqualified; it makes them tempered and prepared to move ahead.

Leadership Lessons Lived is written as an encouragement to continue developing the leadership skills necessary to lead in hard times. Throughout history leaders who came out victorious came out knowing that they had paid a heavy price. Leaders can't rely on past victories and accomplishments. They understand they may have been called to lead an organization during a transitional time versus leading an organization through growing pains or a project. They know their skill set may not be enough or may need to be different to lead their people and organizations to the next level. We will discuss this more, but let's suffice it to say that there will be a next level in the next time.

During your journey I encourage you to always remember that leadership is about people. It is about helping, restoring, strengthening and supporting people. It is about listening, caring, and remaining calm. It is about developing endurance and a pace which is manageable. And finally, it's about you and the development of your character.

There always remains a place for you as a true leader. Nations, organizations, and people will always be in search of and in need of a true leader. Continue to prepare yourself and get the rest necessary to be effective for the seeker. There will always be a place for you to impart the "leadership lessons" you have lived. People will recognize you and come along side of you. They will sacrifice for you and walk with you as long as they know you are with them with all your heart

You will have your own experiences behind you to encourage others to live their own leadership lessons. Please share them with us, and together we can build stronger men and women who truly have the best interest of their people in mind. Enjoy the journey and take time to enjoy your people. And of course, last but certainly not least...

Don't just learn the lessons; live the lessons.

CONTENTS

CHAPTER 1

LIVING THE LESSONS LEARNED

Success is dependent on effort. -Sophocles

I have joked many times about my first book on leadership being lessons learned and not always lived. The truth in the joke is that it can't be a joke. Leadership realities require us to walk the talk. How many of us have met people who seem to talk a good talk but can't walk the walk. A leader doesn't need someone to tell them they are a leader; people recognize leaders. They also recognize people who are in leadership positions and seem ineffective. Those people are either wrong for the position or are ill-equipped for handling the role. I have met many in these positions whose hearts are in the right place, and they desire to do well and endure the job and then go home wondering what just happened. Some can be oblivious to the fact that they don't have the skills necessary to be a good leader. They think that just because they are in the position that they are truly a leader. True leaders don't need a position. The position will find them. We all have read the books describing the many different types of leaders, and still I find leaders referring to themselves as managers.

You have to wake up and be alert to know that you are always leading. You can't separate yourself from the position of leader because it is who you truly are. It would be like a person with the title of Division Director on their office door entering their office and behaving like a secretary in need of direction. Most of such a leader's subordinates would see that leader as crazy. Then they would question why they are following that person when they should be following that person's leader. You aren't a leader just because the title was bestowed on you.

You also can't stop living the lessons because the weekend arrives. People look to you to be who you are in every aspect of your life, and you should feel the freedom to walk as the leader you truly are and not as somebody needing approval and permission.

People can sense when someone is selling them a bill of goods. They will soon find out if we have walked the walk or are simply just talking the talk. I personally would be afraid to lead a group of people in a direction I know absolutely nothing about. That's not to say I haven't or wouldn't but those times were scary, and I sought counsel and always stood firm comforting my people and staying out in front for them.

Leadership Lesson Lived: Walk the talk and live the lesson

Chapter 2

BEING SECURE IN YOUR CALLING

Somehow we learn who we really are and then live
with that decision.
-Eleanor Roosevelt

I have witnessed and also found myself looking around and seeing who was going to give me the acknowledgements that I was so desperately looking for because times were hard, and my staff didn't like what they were hearing. I watch as I listen to other leaders speak on this topic and they look into the audience for someone whose head is nodding in approval at what they are saying. You don't need that approval. Say what you have to say and leave it at that. Yes, you will probably be challenged. So what! As you live the leadership lessons stand firm on the authority of the position you have been given. Does it really matter if everyone agrees or not? I guarantee you that isn't going to happen, and you can also learn something as your own thoughts are challenged.

I have been challenged many times as I have tried to move people out of their comfort levels of mediocrity. I despise mediocrity in my own life, and I definitely don't like seeing it in any of my staff. I have been in several different organizations as a consultant having to tell the people it was not appropriate to be late or misuse their sick time. These were grown adults, voters, tax-paying citizens, mothers, and fathers, all with levels of higher education. I shouldn't have had to tell them these things but because the culture has made it acceptable to be late or leave the office short-staffed, it became necessary. Sure enough some got on board and others were sent packing to help a different organization attain a new level of mediocrity. How would we like it if we sat down at the regularly scheduled time to watch our favorite sports teams play and then had to wait because not all of them showed up together at the same prescribed time? We would feel like we don't really matter to them at all. We would feel that they are selfish. Who does that sound like? Anyone you are leading?

It takes a strong person to stand firm and demand upward movement. We aren't taking a vote, nor are we waiting for everyone to forge ahead. We will lead others into a new culture with higher standards and raise the levels of professionalism, ensuring better service, quality, and care. Let's leave the mediocre professional lifestyle behind us.

Leadership Lesson Lived: Stand firm in your position

CHAPTER 3
GROW UP!

The art of living lies less in eliminating our troubles than in growing with them. -Bernard M. Baruch

As the title suggests, grow up! Enough said? Probably not. Nor is it meant to be offensive. I found myself needing to remind myself of my own need to grow up. We often have thoughts of the way things should be, and when they aren't we throw a "professional temper tantrum." We justify our actions by saying since we are leaders we can act anyway we like. And after all, aren't we as leaders like the proverbial customer—always right? The simple answer is no. The more complicated answer is that no matter how long we have been in a position of leadership, we are always growing and learning that the ways we acted yesterday weren't necessarily the best. Change is in order. I personally believe that with each decade we live, we are still learning to overcome and grow unless we simply decide to stop.

I find most of my immature actions have come as a result of being offended. I find them even being more exaggerated when I am physically and emotionally tired. I have had many other "leaders" go behind my back and "tell on me" like we were in grade school. They would run to my leader and tattle because in their eyes I might not have been fair or their own intentions were misguided. I find that such people have inflated egos and need the approval of their superiors. I tell you now that I don't seek or need the approval of my superiors. I want to know if I am meeting their requirements and being who they need me to be, but usually my standards are higher so that isn't even a worry.

The most mature leaders I have admired from a distance have learned to hold their emotions in check. They have made a conscious decision not to respond in an undignified manner. We have all seen political debates and news talk shows that get attention because this or that person was angry and lashed out by yelling, screaming, or calling someone names. What is sad about this is that it is what we actually remember about them, rather than their opinions or ideas. We can't remember their stance on issues or even the subject of the debate. It makes for good television; it doesn't make for good leadership. Often I find myself embarrassed for them.

Just because we think something doesn't make it right. Just because we are in a position of leadership doesn't mean we don't have to grow up. It's not all about us. When we act like it is, we have failed to make the necessary adjustments.

Leadership Lesson Lived: Leaders choose to plan and monitor their growth.

Chapter 4
ALWAYS AN ANSWER

Be kind for everyone you meet is fighting a hard battle. -Plato

People need answers. They often look to national and international news sources to get them. They have been led astray, disappointed, and burned by misguided and outright deceptive leaders. People tend to follow a personality who is outgoing, appears confident, dresses well, and tells them what they want to hear. The willingness of people to follow anyone who meets that simple set of criteria has caused many to fall and left many in financial ruin. A good leader isn't someone telling people what they want to hear, but one who is telling them what they need to hear. Most people will accept what you have to say as long as it is the truth. They may not like it and may reject the philosophy on which it is founded, but they will accept it within reason.

A leader always has an answer or the ability to discover it. There is a biblical scripture in 2 Timothy 4:2 "Preach the word. Be prepared in and out of season; correct, rebuke, encourage with great patience and careful instruction."

For centuries leaders have had this wisdom. If you read the biblical passage carefully you will see that those characteristics of patience and care are used almost daily in your interactions with others. I want to point out that you can't always have an answer without being prepared. When does it mean to be prepared? Only on Tuesdays and every other week? No, it means to be prepared in and out of season. What does that mean? To get your answer, you have to understand seasons. A season refers to a period of time. Most of us think in terms of spring, summer, autumn, and winter. But there are many different seasons. Retailers know that they have to sell baseball items in the spring and summer because they won't sell many in the winter. Flower growers know that lilacs bloom in the spring, but they grow them in all seasons. We prepare for winter during the summer and fall. Farmers don't wait for the planting season to make sure their equipment is ready to go. They prepare ahead of time.

What am I saying? Always have an answer because the season is either coming or it's here now. Businesses are always doing research and looking for the latest and greatest technology. Are you prepared to give them an answer? A good analogy in thinking about being prepared is this: it's too late to prepare for war once war is upon you. People are always looking for an answer. They are always looking to their leaders for those answers. Because of this constant quest for answers, leaders must think for themselves because so many people ask the television and others to tell them what to think. That is lazy. Prepare yourself to have answers before the answers are ever needed. People may not like your answers, but at least you have a response you have thought about, and you can appear as if you are in control

Leadership Lesson Lived: Be prepared in and out of season with an answer.

Chapter 5
EVERYONE'S FROM SOMEWHERE

Give to the world the best you have and the best will
come back to you.
-Madeline Bridges

We all struggle with confidence at times. I have never met someone who was born totally confident or who was accepted everywhere he or she went. When I wrote my first book, I struggled as I asked myself who in the world would want to read what I had to say. But I felt in my spirit and heart that I was supposed to write the book. However, I didn't know the who, what, why, where, and when's of writing it. I knew I had to get the book out and say what I needed to say, and since much of it was personal and filled with failures as well as success, I kept fighting self-doubt and wasn't confident I could pull it off. Then one night at dinner, I was sharing with my family my internal struggle. I asked them the following question. "Why would someone want to listen to me and read my book?" "Why would someone want to listen to a guy originally from rural Missouri?" Suddenly my daughter spoke up and said, "Dad, everyone is from somewhere." I fell over in amazement when I realized the maturity my daughter was expressing to me. We can all list excuses for why we should disqualify ourselves even before we are exposed to the ruthless court of public opinion—the court that holds nothing sacred. Instead we should be listening to our own inner spirit bearing witness that we are to respond to what God has called us to do and leave the rest to him.

We all have times in our lives when we haven't responded or performed admirably. What I want to encourage you to do as a leader living these lessons is to keep your confidence in a safe place and not hand it over to anyone.

Confidence isn't an option. Confidence isn't arrogance in disguise. Confidence is accepting the surety of the who, what, where, and whens at times when we can't see and don't have all the answers. Someone is watching you as a leader. Stand firm in the face of critics, judgments, bad press and personal failures.

We all have something to say and something to contribute to this great world we live in. This leaves us with the only response we can give and that's obedience to our special calling. We don't have to save the earth from extinction, but we do have to be persistent and realize we are like others in the world; we are all from somewhere with something to contribute. Live this lesson well.

Leadership lesson lived: No matter what your beginnings were, you have something to contribute to the world for a lifetime.

CHAPTER 6

YOUR BUSINESS WILL TAKE ON THE LEADERS PERSONALITY

The secret of success in society is a certain heartiness
and sympathy.
-Ralph Waldo Emerson

I have gone to many hospitals and healthcare organizations and spoken with leadership who have asked me to come and help during times of crisis. May I first of all say how much of a privilege it is to be entrusted with the people an organization holds so dearly. Most organizations understand that their people are their greatest asset.

I find it amazing that though they know that their staff is their greatest resource, they are often also the resource they invest the least in, in terms of growth and education. We live in such a "what have you done for me lately" society with a "what can you do for me right now" mentality that we haven't realized how much it has affected us in terms of retaining employees.

Most employees desire a workplace that is a home away from home that they can invest in and have it invest back in them. Employees know that, just as families go through hard times, they may have to suck it up and pull the financial belt tighter for their company, and they are usually willing to do so if they believe in the organization.

Sometimes I go to an organization that has a high turnover rate, but the company has no idea why. Senior leadership think it is solely the responsibility of the manager of the unit to retain employees and don't take any responsibility for the attrition. They often hand down the "rules" and expectations and give little to no input into a manager's growth. Then they sit back and have meetings trying to figure out why things have gone wrong.

One reason is because the unit has taken on the values and personality of the leader. How often have you tried to communicate with a leader from a different unit and found them to be allusive or uncaring and then tried to relate to their staff only to get the same response? How many customer surveys will you continue to read with the same issues time and time again before an action is required? We have focused so much on the financial aspects of the organization that often we forget to refocus on the healing necessary for our people who have been on the front lines of the fight.

You also have to focus on the obvious points of not just hiring someone who has a pulse. You have to make the right hires. You can do all the personality tests you want to trying to make the right fit and can still miss out on the right hire.

Look at what the desired result is for the season you are in and hire the right person that will lead your organization and unit into the future you desire.

Leadership Lesson Lived: Your organization or department will take on the leader's personality including the good and not-so-good aspects.

CHAPTER 7
LEAD FROM THE HEART

I don't go by the rule book. I lead from the heart not the head.
-Diana, Princess of Wales

How many times have you read advice from some of the leadership experts that didn't quite work? One thing you will learn or probably have learned is that no two organizations are the same. As we read in a previous chapter, an organization often takes on the personality of its leadership. That can be a good or not-so-good. When it isn't a good thing, we usually see that the leader isn't leading from their heart but from what they think is right. That's the trap. I learned a long time ago that just because I think something, it doesn't make it right. Often our thoughts appear correct until we allow them to be challenged. What then does a leader do when the books and advice he or she has read and taken don't seem to work? Quite simply, she or he must lead from the heart.

Leading from the heart isn't a bad thing or an emotional thing. It is the primary thing. When people are your priority, your heart centers in the right place. That doesn't mean that people can just manipulate you or that you have the most expensive health plans and bow to every employee's opinion.

Leading from the heart means you take into consideration the best thing for the employees and the future of the organization. We all know that an organization can't exist without good finances and a strong market and vision. We also know that even though you lead from the heart there will be times that people will be hurt. It's inevitable. Sometimes downsizing and layoffs are a decision that makes even the strongest of leaders feel like they have let everyone down. That simply isn't the case. I have been on the down side of a downsizing. I was a faithful worker in an organization for 5 years and had more sick time accumulated than 90 percent of the people who had been there longer than me. I didn't call in, and I showed up on time. The company decided they wanted to go with a more professional staff, and I didn't have a college degree at the time, so I was let go. It wasn't based upon seniority or faithfulness or anything but the fact that they needed to let go of 250 employees. It wasn't fair, but as leaders we know "fair" doesn't always fit into the equation. I was hired back into that same system 6 months later and ended up spending nearly 20 years of my career there. The layoff affected me but just for a short time. My point is that the leaders of the organization made a decision with both their minds and hearts that if the organization was going to survive then a layoff was inevitable. I found out later that at the time the business only had 2 days worth of cash on hand. They were nearly financially bankrupt and had to make heart-wrenching decisions.

The organization's leadership liked people and liked their employees. Their hearts were hurt over having to layoff people they liked and knew were good people who didn't deserve what was about to happen to them.

The lesson to live is to always lead from the heart. Make the best decisions you can and have the best interest of your employees in mind when making decisions, even when those decisions are painful or difficult.

Leadership Lesson Lived: Lead from the heart. People tend to give you a lot of grace when you make a mistake if they know your heart is in the right place.

Chapter 8
GOOD ENOUGH ISN'T

Tis no shame to follow the better precedent. -Ben Johnson

I have many friends like you reading this chapter that I have great discussions with. I love to hear others opinions on ideas and concepts as well as stories of similar experiences we have all gone through. I will never tell you I know it all. I will also not hang around anyone who tells me that he or she knows it all. I don't believe we have all the answers, although I do believe we can create or seek the answers we desire. One day I was having a discussion with a friend about employee behavior and attitudes and getting people out of their comfort zones. It was like we were stuck in the mundane, and my staff lacked the intensity and sense of urgency that was necessary for an upcoming inspection by the largest healthcare inspecting agency of the time. I was discussing this lack of urgency with him when he told me he lived by a motto of "good enough isn't."

I loved the simplicity and power in that statement. How many of us have received service at a restaurant or company that was just good enough? I hate to say it but most of the time I get average to below average service. When I get great service, I'm usually surprised and so is the person I gave my tip to because it is more than they expected. I am known at one restaurant as the person you want to wait on because I tip so well. The word TIPS is derived from old English, and it stands for "To Insure Proper Service." When it was coined the wealthy who came into the city would often have their servant go tip one of the people looking for work to ensure and insure they got great service. They actually paid the tip in advance. What would happen if we did that today? I have tried it and actually gotten taken care of really well. I called my waiter over and showed him in advance what was his if my glass or coffee mug stayed full during my time there. I love good service. I love giving good service. I love giving more than is expected of me. I feel a reward in doing just that. That says a lot about me as a person and about my character.

Leadership Lesson Lived: As a leader always be more than your people expect and understand that good enough isn't good enough.

Chapter 9

THERE IS A SHORTCUT TO LEADERSHIP

Success is simple. Do what's right, the right way, at the right time.
-Arnold Glasow

I am sure as you were reading the title you instantly thought of a phrase many others have told you. That phrase is, "there is no shortcut to success." Well I want to dispel that rumor. There is a shortcut. I discovered this by listening to others who had been where I wanted to go. If you don't believe there is a shortcut then why do you attend conferences and buy books?

You see those things written by leaders who have gone before us can be tools for our own success. I can read a book by strategists of the past and futurists with ideas and discern and learn things from them. Why wouldn't I buy a book and read what those authors went through and prevent myself from making the same mistakes? I can also discern valuable tips that will shorten my path to the success I desire. By reading an autobiography of a successful leader you can learn in a 2 days what took them 20 years to learn by experience. Therein lies the shortcut.

You should be reading books and listening to tapes or cd's or watching DVDs produced by leaders who have paid the price to get the success you desire. Learning doesn't stop when you graduate with a degree. It has simply just begun. The college or technical degree is your proof you have met the minimum qualifications to be in the field of expertise you are entering. Continuing a lifetime of learning allows you to build a future you can't even see at this point in your career.

I also want to clarify one more thing. Taking a shortcut in learning and taking a shortcut when your people are on the line are two different things. You can learn from a book very quickly and you can destroy a career very quickly. Don't be hasty when it comes to making decisions that involve the lives of others. You will be faced with many decisions that others who have gone before you may not have the answer for. Don't panic. The answer is always there for someone who is willing to pay the price to get it. So take your time when making big decisions involving others. You don't want to live with regret. You want to live with peace of mind. The shortcut I speak of is one that helps you avoid pitfalls and allows you to navigate the career you desire.

Leadership Lesson Learned: My shortcut to success is built upon learning from leaders who have gone before me.

CHAPTER 10
KEEP MOTIVATING

Ahh but I was so much older then; I'm younger than that now.
- Bob Dylan

I have found there are keys to managing and motivating employees. Employees want to be valued. They want to know a leader is in their corner when all seems to be going against them. They want a leader who they know will identify with them and one they can identify with. That's called credibility. They like knowing you have been in the trenches with them. You can lead people older and younger than you simply because you have credibility. When I was a new nurse straight out of school, there was no way those who had been in the profession for years would listen to a green freshly graduated RN, especially since they had forgotten more than I still had to learn. Life is odd. When you are young you want to be older, and when you are older you desire to be young again. Hence my Bob Dylan quote. But the thing about managing and motivating isn't an age thing. It's a maturity thing. Sure a lot of times maturity comes with age, but I have found maturity also comes quickly by experiencing life and effectively dealing with issues that arise. I have found younger people who actually act more mature than their older counterparts. But there is a contrast here as well. I like the fact that the older I get, the younger I feel like acting. No one likes to follow a leader who acts like they have one foot in the grave or can't keep up with current society.

Motivating simply requires that we observe what drives and values lie deep within our employees. It doesn't mean you can motivate everyone. I have had employees that I couldn't motivate if I had handed them a bag of gold. There are others I would love to have motivated to leave. Yes, there are those in every organization who take and never give. Their eyes are always centered on themselves alone, even at the expense of the organization and their fellow employees.

Motivating requires a spirit that is motivated. I don't have many bad days. I have bad moments that I don't allow to define my day. In all honesty, I have been motivated to turn and run myself, but I have stayed the course because I cared about relieving the pain of others. I motivate myself. If I need more than what I have, I look for it in my spiritual relationship as well as friends, magazines, and books.

Leadership Lesson Lived: People want to be motivated.
As a Leader, I'm that motivation.

Chapter 11
GREAT LEADERS RETAIN EMPLOYEES

There is no strong performance without a little fanaticism in the performer. -Ralph Waldo Emerson

Contrary to popular belief retaining employees isn't as hard as you have been led to believe. I could probably write a book on this one chapter, but let's just stick to a few points. I have been a member of organizations that have retained employees for over 40 years, and I have worked in organizations that couldn't retain good employees for 5 years. The difference lay within the leadership of those organizations. Were all those leaders perfect? Of course not. Were all the employees a good fit? Of course not. People stay in organizations whose values align with their own. You show me an organization with long-term employees, and I will show you an organization that values its people. People will stay in an organization that doesn't even have the best benefit packages simply because they are valued. Do you desire to be leader in an organization like that? Then begin now. The organization isn't simply the CEO, COO, or board of directors. It is YOU! When people speak poorly or honestly about the "management," I am sure the "management" has a name. More specifically a name you may know very well.

I have been in organizations that had rapid turnover. I looked into these and found organizations that ran purely on a wall-street-bottom-line model. Once inside it didn't take me long to learn that money ruled the roost. I understand this in the midst of a bad year or two. But when I spoke to the HR department and then to the employees, I discovered that there was never an employee survey taken to get a sense of where the employees were in the grand scheme of things. I remember interviewing employees in one organization where everyone kept telling me how much of a family they were. I quickly realized that if they had to keep stressing that they were a family, then they probably weren't. I believe they desired to be a family, but they were all so haggard because of the financial strains placed upon them. Obviously there is more I could tell you, but the sad fact is that so many organizations mirror each other in this way. And I have been in many of them. The one thing I know is that if you take away the people and the purpose and deny a process that encourages and includes the people, then you are setting up for certain failure.

My success in retaining employees comes through the tools of listening, caring and empowering them to take control of their career and organization. It's that simple. I led them to recognize and verbalize what they desired and then empowered them to establish a processes that would get them there.

A good organization will lose employees. In fact, great organizations will develop people that other organizations desire to recruit. If an employee decides to stay, it is because he or she believes they can have a long, satisfying career in an organization.

Leadership Lesson Lived: Good leaders retain employees and mentor employees others desire to recruit.

CHAPTER 12
BECOMING A RESULTANT

Put the importance on the bright idea,
not on the source of the idea.
-Jeffrey J. Fox

I was assisting another consultant once when I heard someone ask him if he was a consultant. I loved his response. He said, "I like to think of myself as more of a 'resultant.'" He knew that people didn't always look kindly on consultants. Although he didn't say it he inferred he was trying to produce results. Are you interested in results or money? What motivates and drives you? I personally love results.

Resultants love to see a finished product. They aren't always process-oriented or always visionary. But they do know what the end product looks like and what it takes to get there. They have great ideas but often like to see others doing the detail work. They love the end result. They love a finished product that they can check off their list and move on to the next big thing.

The character of the resultant is to produce results. As a resultant, I don't like loose ends. If I don't have an answer, I find one. If I don't know the question, I keep listening and asking until it comes into focus. The result is important but the process that defines it is just as important.

The people and leaders who can see results before they are in place best define what those results are. However, if a result doesn't bring most of your people along then it probably will have to be rethought. I often use a military example. For instance, if I tell my staff, "Come on lets attack that hill; we can take it! Chaaarrrrge!!!" And I run up the hill only to look behind me and see my staff standing around saying, "Hmmm I think we can take that hill....Howard seems to think we can...hmmm...maybe..." Then as a leader I have to turn around and go back and define the mission and objective in order to bring my people with me who are necessary for getting the job done. The results have to wait if the staff don't or can't see the result before it's accomplished. That can be frustrating to a resultant leader that isn't very process-oriented. But it's necessary. Being a resultant brings the picture and end result into focus. That's the easy part. Being a resultant leader means you have to have the patience and love of your people to lead them into the desired result. That's truly placing the importance on the idea and result not on the leader.

Leadership Lesson Lived: Leaders know that results are important and that the people are more important.

Chapter 13
LIFESTYLE CHOICES
DETERMINE SUCCESS

Do not live your life safely. -Wilma Mankiller,
Principal Chief of the Cherokee Nation of Oklahoma

Many people aren't willing to start small and work up. They think it is beneath them to do menial tasks required to build the foundation for long-term success. I know this because as a young leader I thought the same way. I wanted to be on the fast track to success. The problem was there was no track, and if there had been, it certainly wasn't fast. It was more like a long and winding road filled with challenges. I had to learn that my lifestyle and desire for quick solutions would affect my success.

Your lifestyle may be to conquer and take what you can before the next person gets it. It may also be one of spending all the money you have to dress well and drive an expensive car so that everyone thinks you are a success before your foundation is ever built. The problem becomes evident when you stop to evaluate where you are and wonder why your track hasn't brought you the success you believed it would or at least at the speed you thought it would.

Spenders soon learn they should have saved more money. Hard-charging leaders soon learn they should have changed speeds earlier in their career. Organizations and leaders have fallen into bankruptcy and defeat because of the lifestyles they chose to lead both on and off the clock.

Building a foundation for your life is the most important thing you can do to guarantee yourself future success. Education, with all its flaws, understands this better than any other business. They don't send a child from 1st grade to High school. They build a foundation that seems to get more stable as a child learns to grow emotionally and intellectually. Somehow we think because we finally got that Master's degree that we know it all and should be placed at the top of the organization. That Master's degree was only meant to begin building a foundation. What you learn on the job and in real life actually establishes what you are.

For success, I highly recommend establishing yourself in humility and building on a foundation that can remain stable, firm, and unshaken throughout the life of your career. Seek many advisors whom you can trust and that you know have paid the price. I find a lot of self-absorbed leaders who, because they are in a position, automatically think they are qualified to be in that position and actually think they should be the next CEO. These are nothing more than self-inflated egos that have minimal basis for promotion. They have to self-promote in any way they can find because they aren't able to show results that are based solely on their efforts.

Establish a lifestyle of learning and working so that you can live within your means as debt-free as possible while at the same time building a foundation that remains unshakeable. You and I have made mistakes and paid for them. Now is your second chance to live, learn, and make the necessary adjustments. Learn this lesson well and move forward in success.

Leadership Lesson Lived: Establishing a firm lifestyle foundation stabilizes my career as well as all other areas of my life.

Chapter 14
LEADERS KNOW THE COST AND PAY THE PRICE

Energy and persistence conquer all things. -Benjamin Franklin

There was a time earlier in my life when I ran marathons. I loved endurance running and races were a time when I could show that my training had paid off. I found that when I ran there were days I felt as though it was effortless and then there were days that I felt like my feet weren't moving at all. Many runners have told me they experience the same thing. We all discussed the sport as being very fickle.

One truth I did learn in all my efforts at running was this: you race the same way you train. If I trained well, I raced well. If I trained half-heartedly then my race results demonstrated my effort. You can see this same principle in how your business and/or business unit prepares for whatever may lie ahead. I have consulted in hospitals that hid their flaws from the initial eye of an inspector, but when the inspector dug deeper, the flaws were obvious and often very glaring. It was obvious the leadership and employees didn't pay the price for the success they desired.

Leaders learn to know what the cost is, and they learn to pay the price with the constant communication and effort needed to be successful. I have seen administrations where I looked them in the eye and told them what I needed to be successful only to have them do absolutely nothing but stare back at me. They were administrations that I have called "High Accountability-Low Support." They were not going to be honest with me no matter how honest I was with them. I have even had them not tell the truth about me and yet blame me for the results. Perhaps you are in one such organization now. If you are, let me offer you some advice.

I want you to know there is light at the end of the tunnel, and it is a train. You are about to get hit and run over. So my second offering of advice is this: turn, run, and run fast! Get out of there. As I mentioned in an earlier chapter, culture beats strategy every time. If the leadership isn't making efforts to change the organization's culture, no matter how much effort you put into it, you will only experience minimal results. And you will most likely be blamed as part of the problem or even labeled as the entire problem. Either way, it is a painful ordeal.

I find that leaders who have experienced this almost always blame themselves because they have a high standard of personal accountability. However, they need to realize that the best people in the world can't change that kind of culture. The change has to come from the top down.

I made the mistake of taking consulting jobs and interim management jobs in organizations that just wanted to show on the outside that things were different, when they weren't willing to pay the price to actually make them different. They were cultures of blame and shifting foundations. Their leaders couldn't lead themselves out of a wet paper bag without blaming the one who got the bag wet in the first place.

So wherever you are, understand that you must realistically count the costs and then assess to see if you and the organization are willing to pay the price necessary for success.

Leadership Lesson Lived: I will always count the cost before taking a job no matter how badly I may want it.

35

CHAPTER 15
IT ISN'T PERSONAL?

Criticism is prejudice made plausible. -H. L. Mencken

How many times have you heard one of these two statements; "It isn't personal; it's just business" or "It was a business decision"? We all understand it may have been a necessary strategic move on behalf of the business, but to say it wasn't personal is only looking at it from one side.

We watch the sports world and see one athlete traded or cut in order to better a team. We hear that it is because it was a business decision. We see a CEO fired after three or four years because of a business decision. What is the one common denominator we see here? It is people. Business decisions have the innate ability to be cold and number driven. But what about the lives of the people that are affected by such decisions? To them it is personal. I told someone once that if it involves me, it is personal. All business decisions have a personal side to them when human beings are involved in the outcome. I understand what is meant by the phrase "It's just business." Many times it is necessary to make human resource moves and decisions based upon finances or performance. I have had to do the same. However, that doesn't make it impersonal to those affected by the decision's outcome. I have also been on the other side of a negative business decision, and that is why I am writing this. I live what I write. This isn't a theory or an effort to sell a book. People can smell a self-absorbed salesman a mile away. I am good salesman. What I write is in the best interest of the reader. Otherwise I could just keep it all to myself. You see, it is personal.

I am living in the revelation that when business decisions based upon finances or plain survival are made there is a personal outcome for someone. I have been laid off during downsizings by the organization I was in that had only two days worth of cash on hand, and I have also had colleagues lie behind my back and cause me pain simply for their own selfish interest. Both situations were personal to me. When we lay someone off or legitimately fire someone, we are setting into motion a law that affects others' lives as well. They may have families and no other finances or ability to recover. Does this mean we don't do it? Absolutely not. We are hired to do what is in the best interest of our organization. Let's just not forget that to someone else it is always personal. May I also suggest that it is personal to the one having to do the undesirable deed and that it affects she or he as well. That person may have to deal with a torn conscience or lack their of.

Leadership Lesson Lived: No matter what decision I am forced to make, no matter how good the decision is or isn't, if it involves another person, then it will be taken personally.

CHAPTER 16

WILLING TO BE MISUNDERSTOOD

In the business world, the rearview mirror is always clearer than the windshield. -Warren Buffett

Make no mistake about it. If you lead people, then at some time you will be misunderstood. No matter how well we think we communicate, it often isn't good enough. We all have a tendency to use a filter when listening to conversations. We seem to have this need to have a reference point for everything. A true leader who is self-aware will learn to remove the filter and listen through the ears of the person actually doing the talking.

However, when we speak we must keep the filter in mind. It doesn't matter what I say if the person listening can't receive it. As a leader I have to find a way to say my message so that people can digest it. That said, I still find myself often misunderstood.

I can truly state that I have the best interest of my friends, colleagues and family in mind whenever I speak with them. I learned a long time ago that it wasn't all about me. When I go to work, I leave my personal feelings and problems out in the parking lot and pick them back up when I'm once again on my personal time. I don't allow my personal issues to cloud my thinking concerning the tasks and people at hand. Even though I have developed this skill over time, I still find people who misunderstand me. They think I am just like them, having the same problems and that I am on the same level as them.

We all go through trials and hardships that are common to all men and women. That doesn't place us all at the same place at the same time. We all are at different levels of life, experiencing different things in each season of life. For instance, I don't pretend to know what it is like to raise a grandchild; I have never had a grandchild. I don't pretend to know what it's like to lead an organization of 5000 if I have only led an organization of 700. As I mentioned in my book *Leadership Lessons Learned*, each organization takes on the personality of its leaders. So if I go into an organization as a consultant and the leaders have been less than honest, then I can understand why the workers look at me as if I were less than honest, even though I haven't been. They associate me with the leaders who brought me in and then filter everything I say with skepticism. My motives and every word I say are met with skepticism and often with anger. I tend to be accused of siding with the administration when all I simply did was convey the truth as I saw it or understood it.

Leaders have to be willing to be misunderstood. It is a hard lesson that is tough to learn because good leaders tend to give everything they have in order for others to be successful. So to have people turn and say you were less than honest or to talk badly behind your back is a tough thing to live through.

Be willing to be misunderstood, but only after you have done everything in your power to convey the truth so your staff can understand you. As I tell all the people I meet that are looking at me with skepticism, time will tell the truth.

Time will tell if a leader is truthful or not; time will tell if a leader lacks integrity; time will tell if what they say they can do will come to pass. Be willing to be misunderstood for the good of your organization. Swallow that tough pill and lead on. There isn't one true leader who hasn't been misunderstood, whether it be a parent or a CEO. The lesson lived is that being misunderstood didn't stop them from moving forward. They could still look themselves in the mirror and know they did the right thing.

Leadership Lesson Lived: Be willing to be misunderstood and don't take it personally if you have the best interest of people at heart.

Chapter 17
LIVING THE LESSONS

Life is a long lesson in humility. -James M. Barrie

I have written the lessons because I have lived the lessons. Anything of mine you read isn't some ideological nonsense. A lesson I learned years ago was that when I made it through the refining fires of life, there was no arrogance left in me. The fire burned off any dross that made me think I was great. I was just happy I made it through those fires. I was alive to live and learn another day.

That lesson is the one lesson I desire every leader to live and learn. True humility will give you a seat before presidents, kings, and men and women of all walks of life.

I am around so many arrogant leaders who have become more than they ever dreamed they could have. Then they astonishingly portray the arrogance of thinking they did it all because they were so great. True leaders don't think they are great; they live great! History and time will decide who is great and who isn't. I prefer to do great things but allow others to accept the glory. I don't need it. My ego isn't so self-absorbed that I need someone telling me how great I am or was. True leaders know who they are and where they are headed without anyone flattering them. Leaders understand that flattery is an insult. It means that the person doing the flattery is too cowardly to tell you the truth and is actually flattering you because they have a self-serving motive.

Humility isn't a bad thing, and it's not the same as being humiliated. Be willing to be humble but don't ever humiliate another person publicly. Leaders should never believe they have that kind of power nor should they ever be given that kind of power. It's not really power at all. It is the easiest thing a person can do as it takes much more effort to invest in people rather than belittle them.

As you learn the lessons, make the conscious choice to live them. Yes, it's true; most lessons you learn as you live them. Life and experiences are truly the best teachers to those whose eyes and spirit are open to receiving them.

As you learn and live the lessons continue to pass them on and share them with others who will care for them as treasured gold. Don't give your best efforts to someone who isn't willing to pay the price as well. Build leaders who will give us a better world.

As a leader and fellow world citizen, I have learned that this life we live is at best very hard. A lot of people don't want to admit it and some even shelter themselves into a lifestyle that is conducive to hiding from pain and relishing in pleasure. I think we have lost track in that the greatest leaders in our lifetime have suffered because we read lessons in a textbook instead of living them out. We forget that in order to make our nation free George Washington slept in snow and bitter cold with clothes that weren't as technologically advanced as ours today. We forget that many slaves have led the way so we could travel on roads built by their blood, sweat, and tears. We forget that many mothers have cried as their children were put in prisons of addiction or prisons forged by iron bars. We forget Abraham Lincoln and the challenge of a divided nation that lay before him as he freed people and tried to bring healing to that same nation. We forget that God sent his son to die for us that we might be free. We forget far too much far too often. Our focus has been divided and distracted. Our hearts have fainted when they should have been strengthened. We have turned away instead of rising to the occasion. We have soldiers who rise to the occasion leading and freeing nations of peoples. God Bless them!

Now is your turn. You too can lead a family, an organization, and a nation forward by choosing to minimize distractions and remain focused. It is a tough job attempted by many but successfully realized by few. Will you be one who is willing to pay the price to live the lessons? Time will tell by your actions.

Be encouraged, step up to success, and build leaders who will secede you, while building on the successful foundation you have laid.

Leadership Lesson Lived: Choosing to walk in humility will save a leader from being humiliated in the end.

CHAPTER 18
QUICK LESSONS TO LET YOU KNOW THAT IT WILL BE OK

First keep the peace within yourself, then you can also bring peace to others. -Thomas a Kempis

This chapter is written to encourage you, although some of the messages may scare you off. I have found as a leader that very few other leaders will tell me the truth as I need to know it. They make everything sound so good that you feel like you are failing if you can't measure up to their experiences.

This much I do know; in the end it will be ok. Read on and absorb the lessons I learned the hard way through experience and not through a book. I have followed the lessons with my chosen responses. These chosen responses weren't always the ones I had at the time, but perhaps I should have.

Lessons Learned:

- People don't always have my best interest in mind. *I choose to have others' best interests in mind.*
- People want what I can do for them; they don't necessarily want me. *So don't take it personally.*
- Expect an intense battle now and forever. *Choose to fight through it.*

- Expect to overcome battles, but the wounds will still remain. *It's ok, and although painful, your wounds heal.*
- There is healing for the wounds if I allow myself to receive help. *Don't be stubborn and hang on to offenses.*
- Getting help is not a weakness; it's intelligent. *Always seek advisors. The top governments have many of them.*
- In life people are in pain; they spend more time outside the workplace than in it, and they bring those personal struggles to work with them. *Look at people the way they need you to see them.*
- Give people the mercy you desire but rarely get. *Mercy pays big dividends.*
- Everyone will reap what he or she sows. *Sow well and often.*
- Press on in faith; it does pay off. *Keep believing in goodness.*
- Leaders think they live principles of leadership they really aren't living. *Hold yourself to high standards and live them.*
- Our egos have a tough time accepting the fact that we may not be as good as we think we are. *That's why we seek to improve.*
- God is on your side and prayer does work. *We serve a loving God you can turn to in tough times.*
- Leaders can't leave out any aspect of life and think they are truly centered. *Life is complex; have yours in order so you can help others.*
- There are a lot of good people and leaders willing to mentor me if I seek them out. *Find the best and establish a relationship with them.*
- Mentors won't seek me out; they have what I need, not vice versa. *Be mentored and become a mentor.*
- Even when I am wronged, the way I respond is up to me. *The quicker I respond correctly, the faster I can move on.*
- There is a thief who is trying to steal, kill, and destroy your career. *Fight the thief and protect yourself.*
- There are leaders who will look you in the eye while being less than honest with you. *Forgive them and move on. The baggage of bitterness is too heavy to carry. Then stay far away from them.*
- There are leaders in positions that should have never been placed there. *I hope I am not one of them.*

- Preparation wins every time. *Be prepared in and out of season.*
- You will fail. *Get over it, learn from it and move on to your next successful adventure.*
- True leaders give their people permission to fail and succeed. *Identify with them in the good times and the bad.*
- Humility governs how success is handled. *Leave arrogance behind.*
- Honor people and don't take them for granted. *You don't know when and if you will see them again.*
- Forgive and forget. *It's ok to forget the offense and forgive the offender; move on.*
- Deal with anger. *Or it will deal with you and you won't like the results.*
- Leaders know excellence is attainable, even in a flawed system. *Shoot for the stars.*
- Leaders know that it isn't all about the leader. *It is about those we serve.*
- Every generation has lived in unstable times. *Be a leader who adds stability to a people longing for security.*
- Leaders stay in good condition in all areas of their lives. *Stay in good physical health. You will need it for the long run.*
- A leader's confidence will be shaken. *However, never let it be taken.*
- Leaders know this list could be endless. *Keep a journal and establish your own list so you too can write lessons on leadership.*
- Leaders leave legacies. *You are writing yours now and may not even know it.*

Leadership Lesson Lived: Live it, baby. Just live it!

As I said, after you have lived the lessons, it will be ok. Keep the faith and keep believing the best and living your best and look out, because you are in for the ride of your life!

Make it happen and make it fun!

Howard

www.ingramcontent.com/pod-product-compliance
Lightning Source LLC
Chambersburg PA
CBHW031501210526
45463CB00003B/1028